A SPIRIT DAUGHTER WORKBOOK

WRITTEN BY
JILL WINTERSTEEN

FOR CANCER SEASON

JUNE 20TH - JULY 22ND

THE NEW MOON

FRIDAY, JULY 5TH

3:58PM PT

THE JUNE SOLSTICE

Every year in the Northern Hemisphere, the start of Cancer Season coincides with the Summer Solstice. Meanwhile, in the Southern Hemisphere, winter is beginning. The cycle of the Sun represents the cycle of our lives and reflects the natural flow of energy moving inward and outward. There are times to grow, times to pause, times to shed, and times to learn. Just as we align with the Moon's journey every month, we can align with the Sun's journey throughout the year with the four seasons.

The Summer Solstice represents the transition from action to nourishment. As the days grow longer, the Sun gives our bodies and the plants around us more life-giving energy. We can bask in the summer glow and recharge our spirits with light. As our physical world is nurtured by the Sun, so is our spiritual world. Summer and the light it brings remind us that there is hope in the world. They also teach us that we each carry a light within that can spread to the far reaches of the globe to inspire others. We can nurture those around us, just as the Sun nurtures us.

Summer is a time to work on ourselves and our ability to emit a frequency of inspiration, hope, and light. It's a time to slow down and nurture ourselves as we find meaning in our journey. Summer is a time to have patience, both with the seeds we planted in the spring and with ourselves. It's a time to understand that uncertainty always exists and that we sometimes need to sit in the space of the unknown to grow. This is the rhythm of nature: new beginnings transition into a period of uncertainty when we don't know how the chips will fall. During this time, it is easy to become anxious about the future. Summer is the time to develop faith in our lives, squash the darkness with light, and trust that, just like the Sun, we will rise each day no matter where our paths take us.

The Summer Solstice is a day of light and a reminder that the light always exists. As we honor the life-giving nature of the Sun, we honor the light within ourselves. This celebration shifts our consciousness into a period of patience and growth. Just as our ancestors waited patiently for the crops to bring them a fall harvest, summer remains a time to nurture ourselves through patience and love. As you walk through this day, feel the energy shift around you as you prepare for the next three months and the next three Sun Seasons: Cancer, Leo, and Virgo. Feel the subtle changes as the energy begins to settle for spring. Slow down and ask yourself what you need to restore your spirit as you hold space for yourself to come into full bloom.

Below are some rituals you can practice on this day to honor the cycles of the Sun as we step into this new phase of summer.

HONOR THE FOUR DIRECTIONS

The four directions—east, south, west, and north—represent the seasons and their corresponding equinoxes and solstices. Through acknowledging and asking the directions for guidance, we align ourselves with the divine, cyclical rhythm of nature. You can do this practice at any time of the day on the Solstice, but it is best done at sunrise.

Have four candles, one placed at each of the four directions (you can use a compass to mark these points). Before beginning, state that you are open to receiving guidance and intuition, and to opening your consciousness. Light each candle as you face that direction while closing your eyes and meditating on that direction's energy. Allow the information to flood in. Continue through all directions, then journal about what each one brought you.

+ East is the direction of spring, where the Sun rises. It represents change and new beginnings. Reflect on what has shifted for you in the past three months and the new opportunities that have come into your life.

THE JUNE SOLSTICE

+ South is the direction of summer. It represents rest, and finding your purpose and direction. Reflect on the more significant meaning of your life and what needs to be nourished with compassion and patience.

+ West is the direction of fall, where the Sun sets. It represents a time to go within, detoxify, and shed old energies. Ask for the knowledge of when to slow down, when to release, and when to hold on.

+ North represents winter. It represents wisdom and protection. Ask for guidance about your life's journey and its evolution. Reflect on your lineage and the road your energy has traveled across lifetimes.

SET SUMMER INTENTIONS

The Summer Solstice is an energetically charged day and an important one for setting intentions. Direct your intentions on the themes of this phase, which are patience, nourishment, and trust. Create powerful "I am" statements that reflect these qualities and the development of them. Include "reception" statements that open you up to receiving the energies available on this day. Examples are "I am open to receiving nourishment and growth" and "I am able to receive the energy needed to develop trust in my life." Set your intentions and continually remind yourself of them all summer long.

_____

_____

_____

_____

_____

EXPRESS GRATITUDE

Expressing gratitude is a good thing to do any day, but especially on a solstice. Write gratitude statements for everything that you already possess and everything that you want to attract into your life. Part of the manifestation process is to actually feel gratitude for what you want before you even have it. Through this act, you are telling the Universe that you trust your wishes will be fulfilled. The very act will call in the energy you desire.

_____

_____

_____

_____

_____

Practice these rituals on the morning of the Summer Solstice and feel yourself nourishing the light within you. Carry this feeling throughout the summer as you align with the journey of the Earth and the Sun. However you choose to celebrate this day, be sure to spend some time feeling the Sun's rays on your face and standing fully in the light of the Sun, just as you learn to stand fully in the light of your own existence.

CANCER SEASON

Cancer Season ushers in a time to slow down, be patient, and feel. The last three months were a whirlwind of energy. They brought us new beginnings and changes in perspectives, and they taught us things about ourselves we had forgotten. Cancer Season is all about slowing down long enough to feel the emotions we have conveniently avoided until now. It's a time to be patient with ourselves, to receive soul nourishment, and to feel safe in the face of our own emotions.

Cancer's energy represents many things. At the heart of it is the foundation for healing. Cancer teaches us to heal, restore, and replenish ourselves. To gain these gifts, we must be willing to feel. Feeling is the foundation for everything else Cancer's energy provides us. We must feel to hear our intuition. We must feel to help others. We must feel to grow into the next version of ourselves. Feeling is the starting point for much of what we want to manifest.

The feeling encouraged by Cancer's energy is raw, untamed, and primal. It's the kind of feeling that makes you scream with joy and rage. Or cry for hours with no reason why. This type of feeling does not ask why or look for points of origin. It just occurs. It comes from deep within, and we might not even know what it's about. That's ok though. Cancer just wants us to feel. We don't need to write a story about our feelings or explain their occurrence. We don't need to fix them or make them go away. We just need to be present with them.

Over Cancer Season, invite your feelings into your space. Resist the urge to explain them away or suppress them. Suspend using methods that calm you down for this season, and let your feelings have a moment to just be. You can always settle your system if needed. But attempt to give yourself open space, where your feelings can roam free and you simply stand in their presence.

CANCER SEASON

When we stand in the presence of our feelings without trying to avoid, suppress, or fix them, we let ourselves know it is ok to feel. When we can sit with our tears and hold ourselves through turmoil, we tell our energy that we are safe even if we are experiencing wild emotions. Through presence, we learn that it is ok to have emotions and it is ok to express those emotions. We also tell ourselves that we are still loved and cared for no matter how we feel. This permission opens doors to our intuition, healing, and ability to give to others.

Over this season, allow yourself to feel. Notice if you feel safe when your emotions arise. You can even practice telling yourself you are safe when emotions sweep over you. Notice if you attempt to suppress emotions because they scare you or you were never taught it was ok to feel. Take this opportunity to allow yourself to feel safe in your emotions and know that when you do, they pass with greater ease, giving way to your deeper knowledge.

Along with a time to feel, this season is a time to hear your most intuitive self. Intuition comes from deep within your consciousness. It is not tied to logic or practicality. You cannot prove it, and you cannot test its validity before acting on it. When you don't honor your intuition, it feels like an act of betrayal. Your intuition is the part of yourself that already understands the future and the past. It's the part of your energy that extends far past your physical body and connects to the Universal wisdom, bringing you insights and revelations.

Intuition, though, comes from feeling. You cannot think it, and if other emotions are in the way, it can become blocked. When you suppress your feelings, you suppress your intuition. It has no outlet to be felt, and you have to navigate life without it. You cannot decide what to feel and what not to feel. If you choose to ignore or suppress your emotions, the doors to your intuition also close. The only way to reopen them is to feel all of your emotions.

Over Cancer Season, practice using your intuition to make decisions. Your intuition does not require overthinking. It comes in hits or moments of insight. It might feel like an "a-ha" moment or a flash of insight. It may come to you in meditation as an energetic download. Or it might come out of nowhere when you are in the shower or driving to work. Your intuition will feel like a wave of knowing throughout your being. It might not make logical sense, but your entire body, mind, and spirit will know that it's right.

While your intuition is always right, it can take some time to hear it and trust it. Over this season, start using your intuition to make small decisions, like what restaurant to eat at, or where to take a day trip, or when to call a friend to check in. Simply ask yourself what to do, and listen to the answer. Don't question it or try to prove it—just listen, trust, and watch what happens. Over this season, it can be helpful to keep an intuition journal. Write down times you listened to your intuition and what happened. Did your intuition lead to a path of serendipitous events? Also, write down times you didn't listen to your intuition, and reflect on how that made you feel.

The best part about listening to your intuition is that it's easy and efficient. You can navigate life so much faster and with more confidence when you listen to your intuition. It gives you the exact information you need when you need it. Over this season, take time for yourself to feel, to listen, and to allow your intuition to lead you through life. Then watch the magic, healing, and serendipity that unfold when you live a life centered in feeling.

TIPS FOR CANCER SEASON

TIPS FOR FOLLOWING YOUR INTUITION

Intuition is our inner compass, guiding us through life's myriad choices and challenges with a silent whisper that often knows best, even when our logical mind hesitates. Learning to listen and trust this inner voice is a powerful journey towards self-discovery and fulfillment. Here are practical tips designed to help you connect with and follow your intuition more effectively.

1. CREATE SPACE FOR SILENCE

Intuition speaks in quiet moments, often drowned out by the noise of daily life. Dedicate time each day to silence and stillness. Whether through meditation, a quiet walk, or simply sitting peacefully without distractions, these moments of silence are when your intuitive insights can surface. As you practice, you'll begin to notice subtle nudges that guide your decisions and thoughts.

2. NOTICE YOUR GUT FEELINGS

Often referred to as "gut feelings," intuitive sensations are physical responses your body gives in reaction to situations or decisions. These might be feelings of comfort or discomfort, a sense of dread, or a flutter of excitement. Pay attention to these physical clues as they are direct communications from your intuitive mind. Learning to trust these feelings can be a powerful guide in making choices that align with your deepest desires and truths.

3. KEEP AN INTUITION JOURNAL

Start documenting your intuitive experiences. Whenever you have a strong gut feeling or a spontaneous idea pops into your head, write it down. Note the context, what you felt, and any subsequent outcomes when you followed (or didn't follow) that intuition. Reviewing this journal can help you see patterns and strengthen your trust in your intuitive capabilities.

4. PRACTICE MINDFULNESS AND AWARENESS

Mindfulness practices enhance your awareness of the present moment and help you become more attuned to the subtleties of your thoughts and feelings. As you practice mindfulness, you sharpen your ability to discern between random thoughts and true intuitive insights. It also helps in reducing the mental clutter that obscures your intuition.

5. ASK YOUR INTUITION DIRECT QUESTIONS

Sometimes, direct questions can provoke intuitive insights. Before making a decision, ask yourself questions like, "What feels right?" or "What is the best course of action?" Then, be open to the first thought or feeling that comes to you. This practice can be particularly enlightening in situations where you feel torn between different choices.

6. USE CREATIVE OUTLETS TO ACCESS YOUR INTUITION

Engaging in creative activities like painting, writing, or playing music can open up pathways to your subconscious, where much of your intuitive knowledge resides. These activities quiet the rational mind and allow intuitive thoughts to emerge more clearly. You may find insights surfacing during or after a creative session that you hadn't considered before.

TIPS FOR CANCER SEASON

TIPS FOR FOLLOWING YOUR INTUITION

7. SLEEP ON IT

Giving yourself time to "sleep on" a problem can result in a clearer understanding of what your intuition is telling you. The subconscious mind processes information differently from the conscious mind and can often come up with solutions that the waking mind cannot. You might find that you wake up with a fresh perspective that feels intuitively right.

8. RECOGNIZE THE DIFFERENCE BETWEEN FEAR & INTUITION

Fear and intuition can sometimes feel similar, but they come from different places. Fear is often more anxious and produces a constricting feeling, aiming to protect you from perceived threats. In contrast, intuition is a calm, often neutral feeling that guides rather than scares. Your intuition feels expansive. Distinguishing between these can help you follow your true intuition without being swayed by fear-based reactions.

9. TRUST AND ACT ON YOUR INTUITION

The more you act on your intuition, the stronger it becomes. Trusting this inner guidance requires courage, especially when it goes against logical considerations or external opinions. Start with small, low-stakes situations to build your confidence in your intuitive decisions. As you see the positive outcomes of following your intuition, your trust in it will grow.

10. REFLECT ON PAST INTUITIVE SUCCESSES

Reflecting on instances where your intuition led you to positive outcomes can reinforce your trust in your intuitive abilities. Recall times when a spontaneous decision turned out to be exactly right or when a gut feeling saved you from a bad situation. These reflections confirm that your intuition is a reliable ally.

11. REFLECT AND ADAPT BASED ON OUTCOMES

After making decisions based on your intuition, take time to reflect on the outcomes. How did following your intuition affect the situation? What did you learn from the experience? Reflecting helps you fine-tune your intuitive senses and grow more confident in your ability to use this inner guidance system effectively.

12. SEEK SYNCHRONICITIES

Synchronicities, or meaningful coincidences, can be affirmations from the universe that you are on the right path. Pay attention to these occurrences as they can reinforce your intuitive choices and encourage you to continue relying on this inner wisdom. Noticing and acknowledging synchronicities can enhance your trust in both the journey and your ability to navigate it intuitively.

The journey to fully embracing and utilizing your intuition is ongoing. Like any skill, it requires patience, practice, and dedication. Celebrate your successes, learn from your missteps, and continue to create an environment where your intuition can thrive. The more you practice, the more natural it will become to listen to and trust your intuition in everyday life. Learn more about how to feel, follow, and trust your intuition in the course "Feeling Intuition."

HOROSCOPES

♈ ARIES

You can't always be out conquering the world, Aries, despite what you tell yourself and what other people perceive about you. Sometimes, you need to rest and recharge...and that's what this season encourages for you. You're likely to be preoccupied with matters of home and family, and could even be moving. At minimum, you'll find yourself trying to strike the perfect work life balance... which of course is an endless pursuit. Notice the days around June 21st and July 21st specifically, as that's when these lessons will come to a head. Because we're experiencing two Capricorn Full Moons this season, not just one...it's a lesson for you around rest that might need some extra focus. Let yourself take a step back.

♉ TAURUS

You have the gift of gab this season, Taurus, with people wanting to talk to you and likely talk about you, too. It's an important time to notice how you're speaking about yourself and others, and the beliefs you have about the world based on those conversations. You're set to learn a lot right now, so stay open to new information that's coming your way. Specifically around June 21st and July 21st, the dates of the two Capricorn Full Moons this season, notice any conversations that stand out and heed their call. You're working hard to understand why you do what you do, and this season is going to give you some concrete examples to chew on.

♊ GEMINI

You've got your mind on your money this season, Gemini, and nothing can distract you from where your intuition is leading. Money is simply a form of energy, and not many people understand that so clearly as you. You have a deep understanding that when energy is exchanged, there needs to be a balance between give and take. You're checking your bank statements and if you're getting what you're owed, and the receipts will be highlighted come June 21st and July 21st. These dates feature each of the Capricorn Full Moons we enjoy this season, and give you double (your favorite!) the reason to understand your flow of resources.

♋ CANCER

It's your birthday season, Cancer! No one knows how to tap into the deeply felt human experience the way you do...even when most of the time you're not even conscious you're doing it. The Moon's energy is subtle, and that's one of your many gifts. There's a special New Moon in your home sign on July 5th, which is one of the best dates of the year for you to make intentions for yourself moving forward. Your season will also feature not just one but two Full Moons in Capricorn, so make note of your emotions surrounding the days of June 21st and July 21st. Your committed partnerships are likely to factor heavily.

♌ LEO

You tend to be the life of the party, Leo, but around this time each year you realize that even you may need some amount of time away from the limelight. Cancer season wants you to step away from the applause and check-in with yourself in private. There's a good chance that you're working on something behind the scenes now that isn't quite ready to be revealed. And even if it's only listening to your intuition, making quiet time to tap in will be critical this season. Note June 21st and July 21st as Full Moons to release what's no longer working in your 9-5 life. This season is all about your spiritual hygiene.

HOROSCOPES

♍ VIRGO

Your friends are needy, Virgo, and they want you to come play! The height of summer always seems to be an especially social one for you and this one will be no exception. The group chat is very busy with fun plans and you might be the one leading the charge on half of them! While you're known to be a hard worker, Cancer season for you is about getting out and about within the broader community. Specifically on June 21st and July 21st, the dates of the two Capricorn Full Moons this season, notice where you're showing up vulnerably within the collective. Don't be afraid to let your guard down with friends.

♎ LIBRA

You're working hard this season, Libra, and there's no way around it! Cancer energy will try to sidestep its way around plenty of issues at the office...but the best approach is to try your best to be direct. Your role at the office can lean very motherly, which many people love and some will try to exploit. Notice where you people please when it's unnecessary to get the job done. Especially around June 21st and July 21st, the dates of the Capricorn Full Moons, you'll be ready to come into your power in a new way. Let your office be a shining example of how stable your home life is, and vice versa.

♏ SCORPIO

Adventure is calling you this season, Scorpio and you might just be hopping on a plane to answer it. Your spiritual quest doesn't necessarily require travel in the way you might traditionally think of it, though. You could be studying for your phD, or finding yourself deep in meditative trances that transport you through time and space. The crux of the matter is studying your beliefs by learning about how other people move through the world. Especially around the two Capricorn Full Moons this season on June 21st and July 21st...you're ready to be confronted with what you believe and why.

♐ SAGITTARIUS

It's an intense time of year for you, Sagittarius, and because Cancer season runs on cycles just like astrology as a whole...it could feel familiar. Whether you're indebted to others and aren't receiving the same support in return or start to get intuitive feelings that it's time to close some doors, this season is one for grieving the past and preparing to move onward. Especially around June 21st and July 21st, the two Capricorn Full Moons featured this season, you're likely to have some big wins financially. Accept the support you're being offered and trust that it will come back around again.

♑ CAPRICORN

You're a person who knows how to focus your energy, Capricorn, and this season... it's all about directing it towards partnership. You're hyper-focused on building foundations that will support you and the people you love, and during this time of year you're more easily able to witness how that's paying off long-term. This is a special time for you especially, because there will be not one but two Full Moons in your home sign! Because Cancer season is ruled by the Moon, it makes the dates of June 21st and July 21st all the more potent. Pay close attention to the relationships in your life at this time.

HOROSCOPES

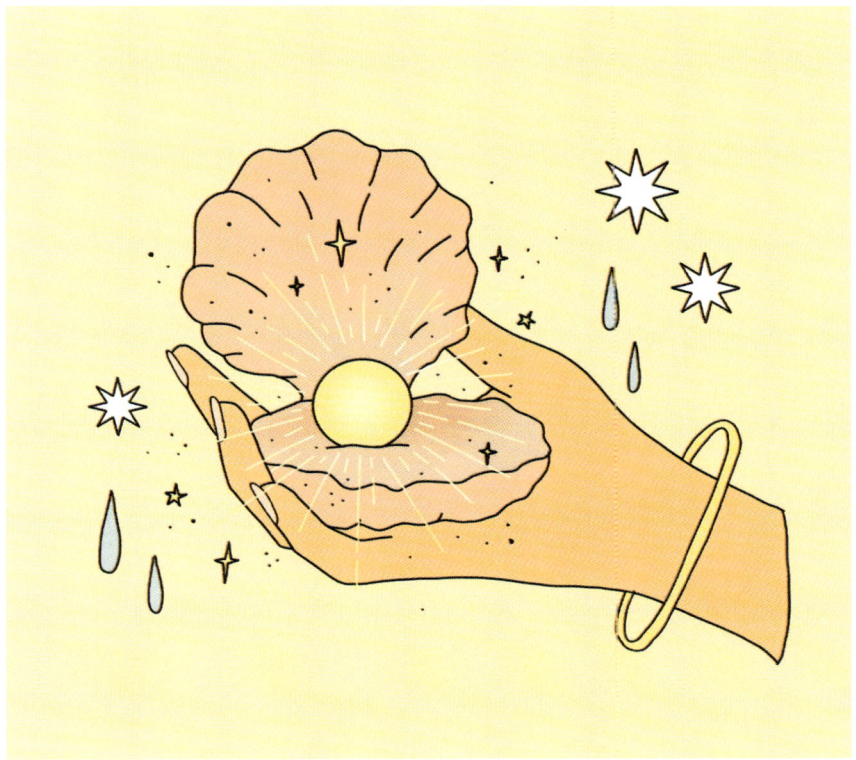

♒ AQUARIUS

You're putting in hard work this season, Aquarius, and all roads might be leading back to your family. For you, the daily grind is about supporting the people you care about most and building a nest that you can be proud of. Not only proud... but safe. You might even be working with family members which of course comes with its own benefits as well as disadvantages. It's important for you to listen to your intuition when it comes to work. Pay attention to your dreams around June 21st and July 21st especially, as you'll experience not just one but two Full Moons in Capricorn. The hard work you're putting in behind the scenes will start to pay off.

♓ PISCES

You just want to have a little fun this season, Pisces...or maybe a lot of it! You might be lining up a lot of fun dates this summer or otherwise wooing yourself with treats and gifts that make your inner-child's heart sing. Let yourself follow the muses that are lighting you up and making you unexpectedly emotional. There's plenty of romance in the air and especially around June 21st and July 21st, you're noticing how your own creativity can help society as a whole. A simple painting you did for fun might just make someone's day and provide comfort to them you never would've expected. Embrace the spirits that move you.

CRYSTALS FOR CANCER

MOONSTONE holds the light of the Moon beneath its iridescent surface. It is connected not only to the Moon, but also to feeling, helping us explore our emotions with ease. Moonstone helps us transition from the logical mind that demands answers, to the intuitive mind that has all the answers. Use it during your meditation to call in your inner guidance and calm your active mind. It is also excellent when emotions become overwhelming. Use it to bring peace as you ride the waves that come with this season. Moonstone is iridescent and ranges in opacity. It often has specks of black, but not always.

Moonstone vibrates to the mantra: "I am all knowing."

SODALITE is the stone of truth. It helps you look past your emotions and find certainty in any situation. It is excellent to have during a discussion or a debate, as it allows both parties to recognize the real details and let go of hidden agendas. Have it with you this season when you are sharing energy with others. It will help you express your true feelings and, in turn, encourage the other person to share theirs with you. Sodalite is blue with specks of white.

Sodalite vibrates to the mantra: "I hold truth."

SELENITE is a powerful tool for removing negativity. It removes lower vibrations from your home, other crystals, and even your own energy field. In its removal, it clears the path for new, supportive vibrations to enter and encourages the overall flow of energy circulation. It will also protect you from psychic attacks, shielding you from other emotions and energy so you can be free to sympathize with others without taking on their energy. Try placing your smaller crystals on a Selenite plate or near a Selenite stone to cleanse them. Selenite is milky white.

Selenite vibrates to the mantra: "I am clear."

ROSE QUARTZ carries the frequency of unconditional love. It brings about compassion and understanding and can help you tap into your heart's messages. Have some near you when you want to make heart-based decisions. Rose Quartz can help you understand what it is you love and how to bring more of that energy into your life. It can also help you give love to others when they are in need. Energetically, it is very cooling and can be beneficial if you are experiencing heat in your body in the form of anger or frustration. If this is the case, hold some while meditating or place a piece on your forehead. It's also great to rub on burns of any kind, including sunburn. Rose Quartz is light pink.

Rose Quartz vibrates to the mantra: "I am love."

RHODONITE is deeply connected with the heart space. It is very beneficial during times of emotional turmoil, as it helps calm and eases anxiety. Rhodonite also supports deep emotional healing. It has the ability to clear negative patterns from the heart chakra and bring peace to your perceptions of the past. If you need heart healing, place a piece directly on your heart and let its energies soothe you. Rhodonite is deep pink and black.

Rhodonite vibrates to the mantra: "I am supported."

CANCER MEDITATION

The Season of Cancer is a time to restore your energy and bring new, supportive vibrations into your world. It's important to give yourself plenty of space, quiet time, and nourishment to process the emotions brought up by this season. Show compassion to yourself by carving out time to meditate daily. Be patient while your body, mind, and emotions slow down as you receive restorative energy.

I AM BREATHING MEDITATION - 5 MINUTES

This is a simple meditation meant to focus your mind and ground you within your body. It is excellent for bringing your mind back to the present moment and gently reminding yourself that your breath is the most important thing.

Start in a comfortable seated posture. With eyes closed, bring your awareness to your breath. As you inhale, say to yourself, "I am inhaling." As you exhale, say to yourself, "I am exhaling." Repeat these statements with each breath for 5 minutes. Allow your breath to be natural. Don't change it in any way. Just observe the reality of breathing. Once you've finished, slowly open your eyes and receive the light around you.

CANCER MEDITATION

LOVING KINDNESS MUDRA MEDITATION

Loving Kindness is a Buddhist meditation that cultivates compassion first for yourself then for others. This particular variation of Loving Kindness uses a Mudra sequence to help focus your mind and connect your entire energy through the use of your hands.

You can practice this meditation anywhere and in any position. You can speak the phrases out loud or silently. For the Mudra, use your dominant hand. As you repeat each phrase, keep your breathing steady and centered in your heart, expanding this space with each inhale.

Begin first with yourself, as you cannot extend compassion to anyone else until you are compassionate with yourself. In a relaxed position, place your dominant hand in an upright position to encourage receptivity. Using your thumb, lightly press the tip of each finger with each word, starting with the first finger. Each phrase is four words long for each of the four fingers. With each phrase, you will tap all four fingers.

PART 1: FOR YOURSELF

Say these phrases three times while tapping each finger with your thumb.

May I be happy
May I be healthy
May I be free

PART 2: FOR THOSE YOU LOVE

Picture the people you love most in your life. Say the phrases below and tap your fingers while picturing those people in their happiest state. You can repeat the phrases for as many people as you like.

May they be happy
May they be healthy
May they be free

PART 3: NEUTRAL PEOPLE

Say these phrases while thinking of people who are acquaintances or people you may not know personally. Picture these people in their happiest state as you repeat the words and tap your fingers.

May they be happy
May they be healthy
May they be free

PART 4: CHALLENGING PEOPLE

Picture people you have had difficulty with in the present or past. This part may be the most difficult, but it will open your heart in new and expansive ways. Recite the phrases and tap your fingers for these people.

May they be happy
May they be healthy
May they be free

Feel free to end the mediation here, or you can do one more round for yourself to bring yourself back to center. Always do what intuitively feels right for you. As you conclude the meditation, take a few breaths into your heart and feel your heart open as your body restores itself.

CANCER LUNAR FLOW

The Season of Cancer is a time to settle into ourselves and allow the body to unravel. We often hold suppressed emotions in our muscles and connective tissue, which contributes to feelings of emotional attachment. To allow emotions to flow freely, we need to release the body and the energy it holds. The following sequence is a Yin Yoga practice, which uses longer holds than a typical yoga practice. In holding postures, you are able to relax into the pose and allow your body to release fully. Through each pose, focus on your breath and use it to keep your mind centered as your body lets go of tension. Also, use props during this sequence: have support ready in the form of a blanket, bolster, and blocks. When we have support physically or mentally, we are more likely to release and let go of tension.

To begin, come to a seated posture, sitting on a blanket or a bolster. Have a timer handy and set it for 3 minutes. For these first minutes, focus solely on your breath. On the inhale, count to 4; on exhale, count back down from 4. Continue this counting for the remaining time. This count is the pace of the breath for the entire practice. Use the numbers to help focus your mind and keep it in the present moment.

COBBLER'S POSE - 5 MINUTES

Bring your feet together with your knees out to either side. Prop your hips up on a blanket if needed. You can also place blocks or books under your knees for support. Gently fold over your legs, then allow your back and neck to relax. Once you are in a Yin pose, just hold it and breathe. There is less emphasis on alignment in these types of poses versus vinyasa or hatha postures. Just breathe, using the counting, and allow your body to unwind. If you are met with resistance in any area, try sending your breath there and ask the resistance to open up gently.

CANCER LUNAR FLOW

ONE-LEGGED FORWARD FOLD
3 MINUTES EACH SIDE

Extend your legs out long on the mat. Sit on top of a blanket and take your right foot to the inside of your left leg. Fold over your front leg. You can have your blocks stacked by your leg to support your forehead as you fold. Allow your spine to round and your head to be heavy. Relax your leg and let your foot be soft. Breathe here for 3 minutes, allowing your hamstrings to open, sending your breath into this area. Slowly switch sides, giving yourself, and your body, time to unwind in the transition.

ONE-LEGGED KNEE-TO-CHEST POSE
3 MINUTES EACH SIDE

Lie on your back and have your bolster or block nearby. Place the bolster or block under your hips, propping yourself up into a slight backbend. Hug your right knee into your chest and stretch your left leg long. Feel an opening in your left hip as you breathe here for 3 minutes. Let go of any tension in your shoulders and neck. On each exhale, feel your body sink into the floor a bit more. After 3 minutes, slowly switch sides.

BRIDGE POSE (SUPPORTED) - 3–5 MINUTES

While on your back, bend your knees and have your feet hips-width apart. Have your blocks nearby. On inhale, lift your hips into bridge pose. Place two blocks under your hips, feeling your entire body supported. Allow yourself to rest fully on the blocks. Have your arms by your side and place slight pressure on your triceps, pressing the floor away slightly to open your chest. Release this pressure and focus solely on your breath for 3 to 5 minutes. On each exhale, let go of tension in your neck and shoulders. Once the time is complete, slowly remove the blocks and set your back down one vertebra at a time, pausing at the bottom.

SUPINE TWIST - 3 MINUTES EACH SIDE

Remain on your back. Hug your left knee into your chest, twisting to the right side. You can place your bolster or block under this knee to give support to your twist. Stretch your right arm out to the side, but keep your neck neutral. Fill your low back with air as you breathe, releasing more into the twist on each exhale. After 3 minutes, slowly come up and switch sides.

SAVASANA - 5 MINUTES

Stretch your legs out long on the mat. Have your palms facing upward in a receptive motion. Allow the entire weight of your body to be supported by the floor beneath you as you rest. Let go of the counting of the breath and breathe naturally, observing the quiet flow of inhale and exhale.

Visit spiritdaughter.com/collections/zodiac-yoga to flow with our Cancer Zodiac Yoga video.

CANCER X THE NEW MOON

JULY 5TH

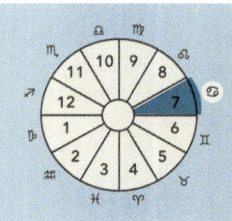

EXAMPLE CHART:

FOR THIS PERSON,
CANCER RULES THEIR 7TH HOUSE

CANCER IN THE: **FOCUS ON:**

1ST HOUSE   Self, your identity, and how you project yourself into the world.

2ND HOUSE   Self-worth, your feelings about resources and possessions.

3RD HOUSE   Communication and how you exchange energy.

4TH HOUSE   Home and how you nourish yourself.

5TH HOUSE   How you enjoy life and what restores your heart's joy.

6TH HOUSE   How you offer your gifts to the world through service.

7TH HOUSE   Your relationships and partnerships.

8TH HOUSE   Your personal growth and transformation.

9TH HOUSE   How you obtain knowledge and respond to adventure.

10TH HOUSE   Your career.

11TH HOUSE   What you are contributing to humanity.

12TH HOUSE   Your spirituality and spiritual growth.

You can look up your natal chart at astro-charts.com.

CANCER X THE NEW MOON

JULY 5TH

Every twenty-nine days, the Moon meets the Sun in the sky, giving us a New Moon. Due to the conjunction of the Sun and Moon, we cannot see La Luna. She has no light on her and travels through the sky in unison with the Sun. They are together as one energy source, and their gravitational pull on Earth is combined. The night of the New Moon brings us many stars in the sky but no Moon to light the way. It is the darkest time of the Lunar Cycle but also one of the most powerful.

In the darkness of the New Moon, the veil between the subconscious and conscious is lowered. We gain greater access to our desires, our fears, and our intuition. We can see the visions of our lives more clearly and understand our future paths. The darkness also softens us. With no light to shine on us, we can become more vulnerable and shed our armor. The New Moon helps us drop our defenses and feel more deeply. In doing so, we can contact the part of ourselves connected to all Universal knowledge.

The energy we hold is part of the energy of the cosmos. It all comes from the same source and has evolved into planets, stars, oceans, trees, animals, humans, and so much more. We are connected to everything we see and can't see through the thread of energy. We are also connected to the past and the future, for energy knows no time. During the darkness of the New Moon, we can feel into the void that began everything. We can feel the connection between us and the vast energy field that makes up the Universe. We can reprocess the past, see the future, and feel into our souls through this connection. We can gain knowledge about what our souls are here to accomplish this lifetime and what we truly want for our lives.

The New Moon is indeed a time to dream, but it's also a time to receive visions. These visions inform our intentions and help us understand the evolution of our energy this lifetime. Each New Moon helps further our growth and illuminate wisdom inside us. The New Moon carries the theme of the zodiac sign it is positioned in. Some signs will show us paths forward, while others may show us paths inward. The Cancer New Moon calls for inner contemplation. This New Moon is about our subjective experience with the world, meaning the way we interpret things, the conversations we have with ourselves, and how much we allow ourselves to open to the magic of the Universe. It is less about doing and more about understanding our relationship with being.

This New Moon is also divinely feminine. Cancer is a feminine sign that holds yin energy. It is soft, diurnal, and receptive. The Moon is a so a feminine energy, representing the side of us that seeks knowledge internally instead of looking outside ourselves for answers. This New Moon in Cancer asks us to receive and interpret rather and do or plan. Allow the darkness to soften you and heighten your sensitivity to the elements around you. Be open to receiving the visions and information coming to you instead of creating them. Feel your way through this New Moon. Allow it to teach you something new about yourself, your life, and your path.

You can work further with this New Moon by understating which house it is transiting for you. We all have twelve houses in our natal chart. Each one represents an area of life. A zodiac sign governs every house. Find the house that Cancer governs for you. This is the area of your life that will be most affected by the New Moon. The chart on the left gives some guidance on what to focus on this New Moon according to the house it is transiting for you.

CANCER X THE NEW MOON

JULY 5TH

The Cancer New Moon is an inspirational time that opens up a portal to our highest intuition, a time full of emotional experiences and deep self-reflection. Cancer's energy teaches us to feel deeply, encouraging us to shed our emotional armor and allow ourselves to fully experience every emotion, energetic shift, and physical sensation. As the New Moon meets this nurturing Cancer energy—its home energy—it can indeed feel like an emotional roller coaster, bringing up intense feelings, dreams, and behaviors.

During this period, the Moon is at ease in Cancer, urging us to find our home frequency. This concept of a home frequency involves identifying a state of being that makes us feel at ease, fulfilled, and content within our lives. It brings happiness and serves as a reminder of our true natures. When we come home to ourselves, we return to the soul—the part of us that remains constant regardless of how our external circumstances have unfolded.

Our home frequency, or vibration, can sometimes be obscured by the plethora of emotions we experience daily. Emotions are transient—they come and go, and sometimes linger longer than they should, leading us to become attached to them without realizing who we would be without them. Yet, it is crucial to remember that these emotions are not who we are; they are merely visitors within the sanctuary of our inner being.

Before diving into the vibrations this Moon provides, it is important to ground your body and mind. Find your center and feel your internal home. You may want to limit mental or emotional stimulation during this day. Find peace by connecting with nature, a few close friends, and yourself.

Cancer reminds us to feel, and this is a day to feel your intentions. It's a time to extend your energy into your visions to embody them, feel for any blockages, and start to materialize them. The Cancer New Moon helps us understand our emotions around our intentions and how they affect their manifestation. If we do not feel our visions are already happening or can become a reality, then we will have a challenging time bringing them to fruition.

As challenging as it may be to face the varied emotions that this New Moon brings to the surface, engaging in this practice is incredibly beneficial. When you allow yourself to fully experience your emotions, you open the doors to your intuition. You cannot truly access your inner knowledge without first navigating the complete spectrum of emotions residing in your energy.

This Moon is also about receiving information from yourself, your intuition, and the Universe. Your Higher Self is connected to the wisdom that extends past the present moment. You are connected to the infinite knowledge of the Universe, including everything that has occurred in the past and future. There is no limit

CANCER X THE NEW MOON

JULY 5TH

to how much your intuition already knows. Any questions you have this Moon about your path forward are already answered by your intuition. Your job is to find those answers, listen, and trust them. This is a receiving Moon. Receive what you already know and let it guide you to your intentions.

Also know that your Intuition is also extremely efficient, providing answers so swiftly that you might miss them if you're not paying attention. The ease with which intuition offers solutions can sometimes lead to distrust, as part of you struggles to believe that answers can actually come so easily.

When you listen to your intuition, you reclaim your power by making yourself your own inner authority. At the heart of this Moon is a story about empowerment. Cancer, the first Water sign of the zodiac, generates Water energy, reminding us that we have the power to generate energy and vibrations that can change our lives and the lives around us—all from our intuition.

As you sit with the vibrations of this New Moon, ask yourself if you have lost your power in some way. Did a past event take it from you? Do you spend too much energy thinking about the past or trying to suppress it? Wherever our attention goes, so does our energy. If we are locked into the past and its events, our energy is being drained by it. We are sending our power to the situation or cycle that caused us trauma and not harnessing that power to manifest our intentions.

Feel your ability to reclaim your power. Ask yourself if you need healing work to find closure to the past. Notice where your thoughts go when you allow them to wander. Notice what emotions come up when you sit with old pain. Are you still suffering? You can feel pain but not suffer from that pain. You may never be able to change the events of the past, but you can take away their power to contain you.

This Cancer New Moon invites us to trust in the simplicity of intuitive answers and to understand that the answers we seek can be straightforward if we are willing to engage in dialogue with our emotions. Your emotions are the key to unlocking the profound wisdom of your intuition. Give yourself space and time to process any emotions, asking why they have surfaced and the spend time to release, clear, or transform them.

In doing this, you create a clear conduit for the energy within your soul to manifest in the form of written intentions. Remember, when speaking or writing from a place of intuition, there is an inherent ease to the process. The answers come rapidly, and even if they surprise you, embrace them. Write them down and explore them further. Often, what surfaces unexpectedly aligns perfectly with your home frequency.

This Cancer New Moon is an amazing opportunity to deepen your inner exploration and plant seeds for a life that truly resonates with your intuition and soul. Let this be a time of powerful emotional honesty and intuitive clarity, a sacred moment to align your external life with the core of your inner being.

SETTING UP FOR MAGIC

FOR YOUR ALTAR OR MOON CIRCLE

FLOWERS:
Lilies, Hydrangeas, White Roses

SCENTS:
Chamomile, Jasmine, Lavender

COLORS:
Whites, Blues, Ivories

SHAPES:
Circles

TEXTURES/FABRIC:
Silk, Silver

ELEMENTS:
Bath with Epsom Salts

Whether practicing alone or in a group, your circle is the container for your New Moon ritual. It helps contain and direct the energy of the night and the magic of the cosmos. Your space needs first to feel safe and supportive. You can choose an area indoors or outside that is quiet enough to allow you to connect with the subtle energies of yourself and the Universe. Before setting up anything in your space, cleanse it. You can use a dried herb bundled in a smudge stick. Great sustainable herbs for clearing are juniper, rosemary, lavender, and cedar. Lavender is an excellent choice for this New Moon, as it brings in a calming energy. Cleanse your space in a clockwise direction, beginning at the most easterly point. You can ask for guidance in cleansing your area from East, South, West, and North. Ask you walk through these directions, be open to any wisdom coming from them.

SETTING UP FOR MAGIC

After you've cleansed your space, begin to set it up. First, anchor each of the four directions with a crystal or candle. Then anchor the middle of the circle with a large crystal, a crystal grid, or a candle. For this New Moon, you can also place a metal bowl of water in the middle of the circle. Allow your intuition to guide you in setting other supportive objects. Incorporate all four elements. Use candles or an outdoor fire for Fire. Use crystals, flowers, or plants to represent the Earth element. Place water in a dish or room diffuser to represent Water. And use sprays or wind chimes to represent the Air element. You can also use singing bowls, as these carry sound through the air. The list to the left can inform your choices on circle items. These elements align energetically with the frequency of Cancer, the element of Water, and the Moon.

If you are setting up an altar, place it in the most easterly point, as that is the place of new beginnings. An altar can serve as a place to set your intentions after you write them. It can be adorned with crystals, flowers, pictures of loved ones, or spirit guides. Since Cancer represents the family, it's a good idea to place images of your family, either biological or soul, on your altar this Moon. After you write your intentions, place them under a large crystal on the altar until the next lunar cycle.

If practicing in a group, gather everyone in the circle after clearing their energy with the cleansing herb. You can wave a smudge stick around them from head to toe, remembering to cleanse the soles of the feet. If you are leading, allow your intuition to guide the circle and follow the flow of the night's energy. Begin by discussing the significance of the New Moon. Then practice the yoga and meditation in this book. Once everyone feels calm, move on to the questions and intention-setting in this book. Give space for everyone to work on the practices themselves, then share them with the group. This is a great time to stretch your ability to receive as you open up with each other and share your dreams.

If you are practicing alone, you are highly encouraged to use the element of Water through a bath. To clear out any negativity, cleanse your bathroom before beginning. Place candles around your bathtub, along with your crystals. You can even place flowers or plants in the bathroom. Gather some dried lavender and chamomile flowers and place them in a muslin (tea) bag. Also, prepare 1/2 cup of sea salt. Mix the sea salt with ten drops each of jasmine and chamomile in a bowl. As you run the bath, place the muslin bag under the faucet to infuse the water. After the bath is full, place the salts and oils in the water. You can even set a few crystals in there as well, except for crystals that end in -ite. Rose Quartz is lovely in the bath. Step into your bath and open your senses to receive the smells, textures, and auric colors of the energy surrounding you.

You can do almost all the practices in this workbook, except the yoga, in the tub. Begin by stating what energies or emotions you want to clear from your field, then dunk under the water three times as a release ritual. You can then practice the meditation. Afterward, relax back with a piece of Moonstone on your forehead, helping to clear your third eye. Lie there for a few moments. Be open to any visions, along with your intuition, during this time. When you feel centered, answer the prompts in this book and write your intentions. Use the Water element to connect with your higher guidance. Remember, you are water and it can connect you with everything you once were and will be. After you've finished writing, repeat your affirmations. You can even dunk under a few times more, giving space for your energy to be reborn as you state your energy to the Universe.

It's time to give yourself
what you need.

- spirit daughter

NEW MOON QUESTIONS

These questions are designed to help you become clear in your intentions. Take a few deep breaths to ground yourself before answering them. Sit with each question for a moment and allow the answer to naturally arise, being open to the person you are becoming. As you write, know you are opening the door to your intuition and giving permission to your highest visions to come out and be seen.

1. What helps you feel your intuition and trust it?

_____

_____

_____

_____

_____

_____

_____

_____

_____

_____

_____

2. What emotions needs attention this New Moon and how can yourself what you need to explore them?

_____

_____

_____

_____

_____

_____

_____

_____

_____

_____

_____

3. Where do you need a container of self-care in your life to fully feel your emotions and hear your intuition?

_____
_____
_____
_____
_____
_____
_____
_____
_____
_____

4. How do you want to feel each day? What do you want to be your home frequency?

_____
_____
_____
_____
_____
_____
_____
_____
_____
_____
_____

INTENTION SETTING

The Cancer New Moon is powerful, inspirational, and intuitive. It is a perfect container for exploring how you want to feel and setting intentions aligned with your soul. This phase of the Moon encourages you to dive deep into your emotions, using them as tools to unlock your intuition and reveal the path to your true essence.

During this New Moon, emotions can range from calm to anxious, happy to sad—all within the span of a day. It's essential to ground yourself, finding peace by connecting with nature, close friends, or in solitude, as this New Moon can feel like an emotional roller coaster. By grounding, you stabilize your energy and prepare your consciousness to engage deeply with your feelings without getting overwhelmed.

Before setting intentions, it's important to process the emotions that surface. Feel into each one, see it, and understand what it tells you about your current life situations and what your soul truly desires. Spend time journaling about these emotions and let them guide you to your home frequency—the core essence of who you are, which dictates how you want to feel each day. This frequency could be peace, joy, gratitude, or another deeply personal state that you wish to embody.

This New Moon in Cancer, known for its deep connection to feeling, provides the perfect backdrop for this emotional and intuitive work. It's a time to be honest and vulnerable with your emotions, to acknowledge and release what no longer serves you, making space for new feelings that align more closely with your desired life. Ask yourself, "Who would I be without this emotion?" and "What life would I live without this feeling?" This process helps clarify your true desires, clearing the path toward them.

As you prepare to set your intentions, affirm your openness to guidance, intuition, and inspiration from both yourself and the Universe. Say, "I am open to receiving guidance, I am open to receiving my intuition, I am open to receiving inspiration from myself and the Universe." These affirmations remind you of your co-creative power with the Universe, setting the stage for a dynamic exchange of energy and intention.

Feel centered in your energy and emotions, then sit down to visualize your future. Imagine how you want to feel and what you want your life to look like. Think about the vibrations you want to experience daily and how you can align your life with your soul's essence. Picture various scenes from your future life that support these feelings—consider the people around you, your daily activities, and the overall atmosphere. What life will make you feel at home within yourself?

Write these visions in detail but leave space for the Universe to fill in the blanks. Focus on the feeling of already living your dreams, not the obligations or tasks needed to achieve them. Notice any emotions that arise when envisioning your future. Address any fears or doubts about stepping into the life you deserve and affirm your worthiness of this life. Make a commitment this New Moon to hold the vision of your future life, to maintain the feelings that represent it, and to always return to your home frequency.

On this New Moon, begin to cultivate a life that feels like home to your soul. Create intentions that support how you want to feel and start nurturing the frequency that will guide your life. Identify the tools that help you maintain this state, consider what you might need to limit, and determine the shifts necessary to support your home frequency. Prioritize feeling good in your entire being, and if something doesn't align with this, be prepared to say goodbye. Make a commitment on this New Moon to hold the vision of your future life. Commit to holding the feelings that represent it and always returning home to yourself.

INTENTION SETTING

AFFIRMATIONS

Affirmations are powerful statements that help you feel that your intentions are real. If you can imagine your visions, then they already exist on some energetic level. Affirmations help you access that energetic level and start to bring form to your intentions.

There are a couple of guidelines for making your affirmations more effective.

+ Write them in "I am" statements.

+ Make them positive. Meaning, do not include "no" or "not" in them. The Universe doesn't hear the negative words, so keep them out of your affirmations.

+ Put them in the present tense. It can be tempting to put them in the future because that's when your conscious mind thinks they will happen. By making them in the present tense, you are letting your mind know they are already happening.

+ Make them specific. Write them in detail while also making them brief and powerful.

+ Include a feeling word. When you include a feeling word, it makes you feel. When you feel your affirmations, your energy starts to feel they are real and begins manifesting them.

+ Repeat them for thirty days. There is a special response in the brain that occurs when we do something for thirty days. The affirmation becomes real in our minds and energy.

For example: "I am passionately sharing my wisdom with Oprah for all of her followers to hear."

+ AFFIRMATIONS / MANTRAS

Cancer

INTUITIVE. PROTECTIVE. CARING. COMPASSIONATE.

PERSONAL SIGNS

CANCER SUN:

People with their Sun in Cancer are smart, stealthy, and wise. They have the uncanny ability to size up a room in moments and instantly know what others are thinking. They are intuitive, maybe even psychic. They have this ability because they feel more intensely than almost any other sign. With this sensitivity comes a power—a power of knowing. They must learn to embrace their feelings, though, and allow their instincts to lead them through life, even when logic disagrees.

Cancer Suns can become overwhelmed by their emotions, becoming numb to them or consumed by them. This sign needs plenty of space and self-care to process their experiences with the world. They must learn to nour sh themselves as much as they nourish those around them. Cancers are the mothers of the zodiac; they love being helpful and needed, but they must be careful no: to put others first. They tend to place their own nourishment in the back seat, forgetting that if they are not replenished, they will have nothing to give.

Cancer Suns are highly intuitive, but they need practice following their intuition. It may take years before they trust their inner knowledge, but it will never steer them wrong. They need a quiet space dedicated to meditation or some other practice that grounds them. In this space, they can hear themselves as they separate from the rest of the world. The space also serves their empathetic side. In solitude, they can feel into which emotions are theirs and which ones belong to other people. Once they understand their emotions and no longer a low them to control their behaviors, they can step into their full power. Cancer Suns will always feel intensely, but they do not need to suffer from these feelings. They can learn to observe them and see them as gateways to their inner knowing, which is always felt.

Cancer Suns are gentle souls, but they also have a fierceness to them. They are strong and ready to fight for what their heart believes. They are governed by the mother archetype and can be quite protective of what and who they love. They are tenacious and have the advantage of their advanced intuition. They are a force of their own, as powerful as the ocean and as stealthy as the crab. Ultimately, though, Cancer Suns desire a stable home, both physically and within themselves. They enjoy people and partners who support them and who are capable of receiving support. They thrive when they can put down roots somewhere and with someone.

CANCER MOON:

People with their Moon in Cancer are both emotional and intuitive. The Moon rules Cancer, so this Moon sign gets a double dose of lunar energy. Cancer Moons hold an abundance of feminine energy, no matter their gender. They thrive when simply being versus doing, intuition makes more sense to them than logic, and they would rather receive answers than find them.

Cancer Moons have an advanced emotional intelligence. They understand their emotions deeply and can help others process their feelings. Cancer Moons are highly empathetic and can understand almost anyone's emotional state. This makes them excellent caregivers, therapists, healers, and friends. They are always available to listen, give advice, and truly step into someone else's shoes.

Cancer Moons must take plenty of care of themselves. They tend toward introversion, so they need a space where they feel relaxed and at home. They need to recharge frequently, and their home environment is crucial for their well-being. They need people in their lives who understand their desire to stay home and who respect their self-care time. The more quiet time Cancer Moons can give themselves, the more they connect with their soul, the seat of their intuition.

ASTROLOGY FORECAST

JUNE 20TH - JULY 21ST

JUNE 20TH: SUN ENTERS CANCER

Every year when the Sun enters Cancer, we're provided with a safe haven to feel our human experience in a visceral way. No longer is it about talking, or moving forward, but simply about sitting still and reflecting. Although, Cancer is a cardinal sign...so there is action involved! It's just usua ly in a roundabout way as this season is anything but direct! Our emotions wo k like the tide: they're cyclical, always waxing and waning. Seemingly unpredictable with a stereotype of being "moody," Cancerian energy really does know how to go with the flow. It's when people don't that things can get disruptive! This season is a great time to practice being your own Mother. Ask yourself what you need to feel safe, what and/or who makes you feel seen and held, and what's your intuition got to say about all of it?

JUNE 21ST: FULL MOON IN CAPRICORN

This season is especially important because there aren't just two lunations...but three. This is the first of two Full Moons in Capricorn this season, and it's made all the more special because Cancer energy is ruled by the Moon– signaling that these lunations will be especially important. This is the first of the two full Moons and marks a moment to reflect back to January of this year. What were you working on? Have you reached the goals you set out to achieve at the beginning of this year? One month from now there will be another check-in related to the same themes of this moment. Make notes.

JUNE 28TH: LAST QUARTER MOON IN ARIES

The last quarter Moon is a moment for release. Happering days before the New Moon, an ultimate fresh start, now is a time to let go of anything that doesn't support the next cycle's pursuits. Because this phase is in Aries, it's all about tapping into our body and our instincts. What is your gut saying about what needs to go? Now is the time to unapologetically say "no" and stop taking actions towards anything that isn't nurturing you emotionally. If you're expending more energy than you're receiving, let now be a conscious moment to say goodbye.

JUNE 29TH: SATURN RETROGRADE

Saturn spends several months retrograde every year, so it's not a shocking moment in the grand scheme of the cosmos, but it does pull focus. Anytime a planet changes positions (even though they never actually do, it's an optical illusion) we feel the energy shift down on Earth. With Saturn, we're talking about boundaries, maturity, and the process of time. When it's direct, we can expect to commit to things long-term and have a practical understanding of what that entails. But when retrograde, this process begins a review. Instead of looking ahead, we might look back at the choices that got us to the impasse we're now navigating. We're reviewing the long-term goals that we have and why we have them in the first place. We might also be doing "stress tests" of the foundations that we're standing on in our relationships.

ASTROLOGY FORECAST

JUNE 20TH - JULY 21ST

JULY 1ST: NEPTUNE RETROGRADE

Like Saturn, Neptune spends about half the year retrograde, so it's not as disruptive a moment as when Mercury or Venus take their backwards turn. However, it's still a shift, and one that will be felt. Neptune is the planet of both spirituality and delusion, always walking a fine line between getting lost and being found. When it retrogrades, we're asked to look at the way we might've been losing ourselves lately– both positively and negatively. In a way, the coming months are about removing the rose colored glasses and seeing what remains.

JULY 2ND: MERCURY ENTERS LEO

Mercury, the trickster of the zodiac, traipses into Leo just two hours after Neptune stations retrograde. This seems to suggest that while some level of our escapist tendencies are subsiding...we've got some grand stories to tell about the adventures we had while we were elsewhere. That's because Leo is the ultimate performer, storyteller, and muse. With Mercury in this sign...everyone begins to share with more gusto. We all want to be the star of the show and the heroine in the fantastical tales being shared (ideally to a large and adoring audience).

JULY 5TH: NEW MOON IN CANCER

No matter the sign where it's occurring, New Moons always bring about an opportunity to plant the seeds of a new beginning. It's when the sky is completely dark and we can't yet see what's ahead that we're able to dream our biggest dreams and make wishes that will carry us into a future that will eventually be illuminated. Happening in Cancer, the New Moon magic is watery and emotional. Rather than thinking about where we're wanting to go..it's all about feeling into it.

JULY 9TH: JUPITER SEXTILE NORTH NODE

The North Node is a potent point in astrology and when planets make an aspect to it, they're communicating directly with our destiny. There isn't a better planet than Jupiter for this conversation, as it's full of hope and optimism...alluding to the fact that we'll be especially excited for the future around these days! We might find a light beginning to shine at the end of the tunnel, and we should practice gratitude for whatever glimmers of possibility that are shining their light around this time. Abundant possibilities are afoot for the future...so pay attention to the signs around this date.

JULY 11TH: VENUS ENTERS LEO

Venus, the planet of love, beauty, and connection, enters the sign of the Sun today and our relationships suddenly become a lot warmer. While Venus doesn't rule Leo, it's quite happy to have a visit in the sunshine. And who wouldn't be? Leo energy leads with the heart and when it comes to Venus, that means our relationships become that much more authentic. Leo is also a fixed energy, so you might find relationships around you settling in and getting more serious around this time. There's a loving honesty in our relationships the next several weeks and the heart chakra is the star of the show. Be open!

ASTROLOGY FORECAST

JUNE 20TH - JULY 21ST

JULY 13TH: FIRST QUARTER MOON IN LIBRA

A first quarter Moon is a beginning. It's a time where the still quiet and imperceivable groundwork has been set, and slowly things start coming to light. It's a toddler's first steps, first words, first bites of real food. In Libra, we're stumbling through the relationship arena and might be experiencing a few firsts of our own. It's important to stay focused on your goals at this time, particularly within partnership. Notice where you're giving and where you're receiving, and where anything might feel off balance with those you love. There's still time to correct the course.

JULY 20TH: MARS ENTERS GEMINI

Mars, the planet of action, aggression, and our ultimate willpower, enters the sign of the twins today...and with it, our desires become two-fold. With Gemini, it's impossible to pin things down, and Mars can be a bit frustrated by that reality. Mars wants to center in on something so it can be pursued and then conquered. But in Gemini, a plan is made...and then it changes when new information becomes available! It's important over the coming weeks to stay open and curious above all else. Getting too fixated on a certain outcome will be fruitless, so instead embrace change and stay flexible. That's the gift of Mars in Gemini...as well as being able to talk your way out of anything!

JULY 21ST: FULL MOON IN CAPRICORN

On the last day of Cancer season, we're greeted by the second Full Moon in Capricorn of the year. Like the first one exactly one month ago, this is an auspicious date. Something that you were working on way back in January is once again being highlighted in a serious way. You've most likely experienced it coming full circle for the past month, and today is when you'll realize this goal in totality. Celebrate the wins you're experiencing right now and trust that hard work always pays off.

LEO SEASON

JULY 22ND

Prepare to feel your inner fire and hear your roar with the help of the brave-hearted lion. Align with this magical season, New Moon and Lion's Gate — with the Leo Season + New Moon Workbook.

PURCHASE AT SPIRITDAUGHTER.COM

HAPPY
NEW MOON!

Thank you to everyone who supported and purchased this workbook.

Special Thanks to Rebecca Reitz (rebeccareitz.com, @becca_reitz) for her beautiful artwork on the cover & pages 4, 8, 11, 14, 18, 30, 32, & 35.

For a monthly subscription contact hello@spiritdaughter.com or visit www.spiritdaughter.com.

Disclaimer: The exercises and yoga sequences in this book are physical activities that should be performed carefully to avoid injury. You agree to accept all risks and release Spirit Daughter and any guest instructors from any and all liabilities. Please take care and enjoy.

Follow along our journey on IG:
@spiritdaughter

We always love seeing your photos & hearing about your experiences with the workbooks! Tag us to be featured on our community page:
@spiritdaughtercollective

The Circle

Join the circle membership in time to begin the Feeling Intuition Course with the Cancer New Moon.

THE CIRCLE COURSES

FINDING YOUR PURPOSE	ASTROLOGY + RELATIONSHIPS
ABUNDANCE	SHADOW WORK
REFRAMING 101	MANIFESTATION
FEELING INTUITION	INSPIRED HABITS
FIERCE LIVING	DEFINE YOUR VIBRATION
GOOD ENOUGH	A MORE MINDFUL YOU

+BONUS CONTENT, A COURSE COMMUNITY,
AND MORE